Wrestling with God

Wrestling
with
God

LifeChange Books

greg laurie

Multnomah® Publishers *Sisters, Oregon*

WRESTLING WITH GOD
published by Multnomah Publishers, Inc.

© 2003 by Greg Laurie
International Standard Book Number: 1-59052-044-0

Cover image by Photonica—Knauer / Johnston

Italics in Scripture quotations are the author's emphasis.
Unless otherwise indicated, Scripture quotations are from:
The Holy Bible, New King James Version © 1984 by Thomas Nelson, Inc.
Other Scripture quotations are from:
Holy Bible, New Living Translation (NLT) © 1996. Used by permission of Tyndale House
Publishers, Inc. All rights reserved.
The Holy Bible, New International Version (NIV) © 1973, 1984 by International Bible
Society, used by permission of Zondervan Publishing House

Multnomah is a trademark of Multnomah Publishers, Inc., and is registered in the U.S.
Patent and Trademark Office. The colophon is a trademark of Multnomah Publishers, Inc.

Printed in the United States of America
ALL RIGHTS RESERVED

For information:
MULTNOMAH PUBLISHERS, INC. • P.O. BOX 1720 • SISTERS, OR 97759

Library of Congress Cataloging-in-Publication Data

Laurie, Greg.
    Wrestling with God / by Greg Laurie.
        p. cm.
Includes bibliographical references.
ISBN-13: 978-1-590-52894-5
    1. Prayer—Christianity.   I. Title.
BV215 .L34 2003
248.3'2--dc21

                        2002152452

03 04 05 06 07 08—10 9 8 7 6 5 4 3 2 1 0

Table of Contents

Chapter One

WHAT IS
WRESTLING
WITH GOD?

If you're ever caught in a freeway jam in Southern California, keep an eye out for me. I'll be the guy weaving in and out in an endless quest for the faster lane.

Or if you're in the ten-items-only express line at the supermarket, I'll be the one behind you, counting everything you lay on the check stand and ready to seethe if I find you're breaking the rules on a day when I don't have time to wait for you.

If you stop to pick up pizza, I'm the guy ahead of you slipping a slice out of the box even before I get it paid for so I can start my meal on the way home.

But you know, I don't think I'm alone. Most everyone I know wants everything—and they want it at the speed of light! It's what we've been conditioned to expect. If a microwave can't cook a turkey in twenty minutes or less, we're out the door. We like our news in thirty-second sound bites. And if we could find a convenient website on-line where we could key in our prayer requests and get instant answers—without ever having to talk personally with God about them—an awful lot of us would try it.

But in spite of all the hurry, every once in a while we'll slow down enough to hear the Lord say, "Be still, and know that I am God" (Psalm 46:10). Suddenly we realize that He is God and we aren't; that He's on His schedule, not ours; and that none of our impatience has any effect on how He works.

I don't know about you, but slowing down like that is awfully hard for a person like me. So I understand the frustration many people have about "waiting on the Lord" and His "perfect timing."

I understand the frustration many have about "waiting on the Lord."

Even when we do slow down, even when we do get to the point of really soaking in His Word and listening for His voice, that doesn't always mean we suddenly get all our questions answered and our problems solved. Sometimes, because of a sudden crisis in our lives, or because of ongoing trials and difficult circumstances (things that can so easily crush us with fear or worry), or because of our urgent need for guidance in some decision we face, or simply because of our craving to see God more at work in our own lives or in the lives of those we love, we get desperate. We get to the point where we can hardly restrain ourselves from going to God and crying out to Him, whether it's an actual vocal cry or a silent pleading in our soul that's too deep for words. We're desperate for a breakthrough, desperate for answers.

It's an experience that some people have called "wrestling" with God. But is that the right way to think of it? Is that really what we need to do at such times? Does He actually want us to fight with Him?

BAD WRESTLING AND GOOD WRESTLING

Sometimes people tell me, "I've been wrestling with God in prayer." My usual response is, "I hope you lost," because if you're trying to bend God to your will, you have a problem. If you're resisting and fighting against His will for your life, you can just forget trying to change His mind. If you're stubbornly persisting in a course of action that you know is displeasing to Him, then you can wrestle against Him all you want, but let me give you a little hint about the outcome: You will lose and lose *big*.

As the title of a Broadway show once proclaimed, your arms are too short to box with God.

If you're desperate for breakthrough, then now isn't the time to fight God—now is the time to surrender. Don't hesitate to humble yourself before God and submit to Him. There's absolutely nothing more important or urgent for you than to stop fighting God and start trusting Him instead. As Corrie ten Boom said, "Don't wrestle; just nestle!"

But there's another kind of wrestling with God that's drastically different. It's a good kind of wrestling, and it's not just for supersaints. It's for you and me, as we keep growing in our relationship and our walk with God.

So how do you tell the difference between resisting God's will and the kind of wrestling I'm talking about?

That's what we'll explore together.

GOD THE GRAPPLER

The most distinct picture of wrestling with God that we find in the Bible is something that happened to Jacob, one of the most unusual heroes of the Old Testament. The Bible tells us, "Then Jacob was left alone; and a Man wrestled with him until the breaking of day" (Genesis 32:24). This "Man" who wrestled with Jacob was not a human being like Jacob himself, nor was he even a mere angel. This was the Lord Himself wrestling with Jacob—and Jacob knew it, because immediately after this encounter he said, "I have seen God face to face" (32:30).

There's a good deal to understand about this incident before we, too, get in the ring with God and try to put a hammerlock on Him. Later we'll look at this story more closely and discover some of the background and what exactly happened. For now, it's important to realize that Jacob was a very flawed human being, like you and me. He had a heart for God, but at the same time he had a tendency to be dishonest, conniving, and downright ornery. He'd spent most of his life wrestling with other people, figuratively speaking—his father Isaac, his brother Esau, his father-in-law Laban, and even his two wives. So when it was time for a truly dramatic, life-changing encounter with God, the Lord came to him as a wrestler.

To a great extent, it wasn't so much that Jacob was wrestling to get something from God; rather, God was wrestling to get something from Jacob.

What was it? *Surrender.*

God met Jacob in this surprising way in order to reduce Jacob to a sense of his nothingness—to cause him to see what a poor, helpless, and weak man he really was. And God's larger purpose was to teach us, through Jacob, an all-important lesson: *In recognized weakness lies our strength.*

A MIGHTY MOVEMENT OF THE SOUL

Jacob's behavior in this encounter with God gives us some good examples to follow as well. This incident is brought up later in a positive light by the prophet Hosea, who says this about Jacob:

> Before Jacob was born, he struggled with his brother; when he became a man, he even fought with God. Yes, he wrestled with the angel and won. He wept and pleaded for a blessing from him. There at Bethel he met God face to face, and God spoke to him (Hosea 12:3–4, NLT).

Like a cameraman using an extreme close-up in a movie, Hosea looks back at this incredible story and zooms in on the picture of Jacob actually weeping as he seeks God's favor. Jacob was a weeping wrestler. And that same intensity and brokenness in pursuing God and seeking to be truly blessed by Him are wonderful things we can learn from Jacob and his amazing encounter with the Lord.

No doubt about it, wrestling with God is something intense and profound.

That's the good side of wrestling with God. For Jacob, it meant that he "prevailed" with God and received

His favor, and it can mean the same for us.

In generations past, this kind of wrestling with God was often described as the quality of *importunity* in our prayer, a word that means being extremely urgent and insistent and even demanding in what we request. E. M. Bounds, one of the great writers on prayer, described this importunity as "the pressing of our desires upon God with urgency and perseverance" and as "praying with that tenacity and tension which neither relaxes nor ceases until its plea is heard and its cause is won."

In *The Necessity of Prayer*, Bounds had a great deal to say about this kind of wrestling with God, and his words are worth reading again and again to grasp his meaning more richly. Here's more of what he wrote:

> Importunate prayer is a mighty movement of the soul toward God. It is a stirring of the deepest forces of the soul, toward the throne of heavenly grace. It is the ability to hold on, press on, and wait. Restless desire, restful patience, and strength of grasp are all embraced in it. It is not an incident, or a performance, but a passion of soul. It is not a want...but a sheer necessity.

Did you catch that?

This "wrestling quality," Bounds goes on to say, is not some mere emotional or physical effort that we work up on our own. Instead it's an "inwrought force"—something inside us that's "implanted and aroused by the Holy Spirit." He equates this prayer power with the intercession of the Spirit of God in us and with "the effective, fervent prayer of a righteous man" that the apostle James talks about—the kind of prayer that "avails much" (James 5:16).

No doubt about it, wrestling with God is something intense and profound, both in how it operates and what it accomplishes.

THE NOISIER THE BETTER?

And yet it's not a matter of how loud you pray or how worked up you get. "This wrestling in prayer may not be boisterous nor vehement," Bounds explains, "but quiet, tenacious and urgent." It can even be totally silent if necessary.

Some people feel they can convince God of their cause the louder or longer they pray. The more noise and commotion, the more effective their prayer will be. But that notion is pagan in nature. That's exactly how the prophets of Baal prayed in their contest with Elijah on Mount Carmel. They prayed to Baal from morning till noon, shouting and dancing around the altar they had made. When Elijah taunted them to turn up the volume, "they shouted louder and slashed themselves with swords and spears, as was their custom, until their blood flowed.

Midday passed, and they continued their frantic prophesying until the time for the evening sacrifice. But there was no response, no one answered, no one paid attention" (1 Kings 18:28–29, NIV).

We can incessantly cry out to God, but that act alone will never guarantee a response from Him. Nor can you demand something from God and expect Him to deliver. Some people teach that when we're praying for something, all we need to do is "speak it into existence," and it will happen. Just name it and claim it. Gab it and grab it. But that approach is wrong.

God is not our butler who art in heaven; He's our Father. No amount of striving or bold presumption will ever get Him to do something for us that He doesn't want to do. Prayer is a *privilege* for the child of God, and Jesus taught us that the real essence of prayer that gets heard is simply this: "God be merciful to me a sinner!" (Luke 18:13).

ALL OVER GOD'S WORD

But that doesn't mean we shouldn't be persistent and persevering in our prayer, even to the point of wrestling at times. What we're talking about is true, strenuous effort in prayer—real exertion, a genuine struggle. That's why wrestling can be a strong and helpful picture for us of fervent, persevering prayer.

In that light, we start to see wrestling matches all over Scripture. We see Abraham, for example, praying with persistent intensity for Sodom (see Genesis 18).

We find Moses spending forty days and nights fasting and pleading for Israel when God was so angry with them (see Deuteronomy 9:25–26).

We see Daniel fasting for three weeks when God was showing him difficult visions (see Daniel 10:2–3).

We find Elijah, pressed to the ground with his face between his knees, praying seven times for God to send rain (see 1 Kings 18:42–44).

We recognize Habakkuk wrestling with God when he kept coming with questions about the strange way the Lord seemed to be dealing with the evil that was all around him (see Habakkuk 1–3).

We see this persistent intensity of prayer again and again with David. In Psalm 39:12 he says, "Hear my prayer, O LORD, and give ear to my cry; do not be silent at my tears"—desperate words like those are all over David's psalms.

Paul practiced this kind of unrelenting prayer, both for himself (as when he asked three times for God to remove his thorn in the flesh in 2 Corinthians 12:7–8) as well as for the people he ministered to (as in Colossians 1:9). He begged the Christians in Rome to pray that way for him: "Now I beg you, brethren, through the Lord Jesus Christ, and through the love of the Spirit, that you *strive together with me* in your prayers to God for me" (Romans 15:30). The Greek word translated "strive together" implies the sharing in an actual struggle or contention—a real conflict.

When Paul saw this level of get-after-it prayer in one of his coworkers in the ministry, he made sure to make a positive point of it: "Epaphras...is always *wrestling* in prayer for you" (Colossians 4:12, NIV).

And then there's the supreme example of prayer wrestling: Jesus in the Garden of Gethsemane. As He experienced an anguish and agony we'll never in all eternity fully fathom, Jesus repeatedly implored His Father in heaven, "Take this cup away from Me" (Mark 14:36).

That dark night in Gethsemane seems to be what the author of Hebrews was thinking of when he reminded us how Jesus "offered up prayers and supplications, *with vehement cries and tears* to Him who was able to save Him from death, and was heard because of His godly fear" (Hebrews 5:7). This was vehement petitioning—heated, intense, forceful, powerful. Perhaps Jesus sometimes entered into this kind of intensity as well on occasions when He spent all night in prayer (see Luke 6:12).

WRESTLING TOGETHER

Persistent, persevering prayer really can become a heated wrestling match, a true test of endurance and spiritual strength that requires our dependence on God as nothing else. For you see, the right kind of wrestling with God means wrestling *together with* Him—and never wrestling *against* Him.

Because the truth is that God always *delights* in answering your prayers and providing for you. Jesus said, "Do not fear, little flock, for it is *your Father's good pleasure* to give you the kingdom" (Luke 12:32). God takes *joy* in giving you what you need; it's His pleasure to do so. We sometimes view God as some sort of celestial tightwad up there who doesn't want to bless us, when the opposite is really the case. True prayer is not overcoming God's reluctance—it's taking hold of His willingness.

> *No doubt about it, wrestling with God is something intense and profound.*

And when prayer requires wrestling, it's never because of any sudden stinginess on God's part; it's because *there's something more He wants to do for us,* something more to give to us, something beyond what we could even imagine at present, and something we could never quite experience if God always answered our prayers according to our own plans and timetables without the sweat and toil of wrestling.

So why does God bring us to that point? Why does

prayer sometimes have to get so heated up and intense and full of struggle?

Keep reading, and we'll find out more of what God has in mind when He leads us out onto the wrestling mat.

Chapter Two

WHY WRESTLE?

Why should prayer sometimes require so much effort?

For that matter, why should we even have to pray at all?

Here's the short answer: *Because Jesus tells us to.*

Luke records that Jesus once told a parable with this particular point: "That men always ought to pray and not lose heart" (Luke 18:1). We *always* ought to pray instead of losing heart.

We all know what it's like to be so overwhelmed in life that we're tempted to lose heart. Doesn't it seem like when problems come, they come all at once? You're sailing along smoothly on the sea of life, and suddenly, without warning, a storm blows up. Your little boat begins taking on water, and you think, *Well, it can't get any worse than this.* But it does. The gusts blow harder, the waves grow higher, and your boat gets more and more swamped.

So what should you do? Well, you can always abandon ship, simply give up. But Jesus has a better idea.

When crisis or hardship hits, we have a choice: We can either pray or lose heart. If you're praying, you won't lose heart; and if you're often losing heart, I would daresay that you aren't praying.

The Bible also says, "In everything by prayer…" (Philippians 4:6). *Everything*. We're told to "pray without ceasing" (1 Thessalonians 5:17), and to be "praying always with all prayer and supplication in the Spirit" (Ephesians 6:18).

Always pray with *all* prayer *constantly* about *everything*—that's what God Himself commands…and there's no better reason for doing it.

If praying were an extremely unpleasant chore (which it isn't) or a particularly tricky and complex task to pull off (which it isn't), that would be one thing. But prayer is an enriching and fulfilling activity, a wonderful experience, and it's what we're instructed to do by our Lord and Master.

I don't think we need any reason beyond that, but what's more, blessings come our way as we watch the answers to our prayers unfold—a loved one's salvation, a divine healing, God's amazing provision in our lives.

THE WAY TO RECEIVE

Another simple reason for praying is that prayer is God's appointed way for us to obtain certain good things. James says, "You do not have because you do not ask." (James 4:2). Do you realize that an answer to prayer is waiting for you right now? The only reason you haven't seen it yet is because you've failed to bring the issue before the Lord.

Maybe you're asking yourself, *Why am I not seeing God's will for my life right now?* Remember James's words: "You do not have because you do not ask."

Maybe you're wondering, *Why don't I ever have the opportunity to lead people to the Lord?* You do not have because you do not ask.

You might be saying to yourself, *Why do I always seem to be just scraping by financially?* or *Why am I saddled with this problem that won't go away?* But have you prayed? You do not have because you do not ask.

James 5:13–14 provides us with a surefire remedy if any among us is suffering ("Let him pray") or if anyone is sick ("Let him call for the elders of the church, and let them pray over him"). The message is clear and simple: When we're in need, we are to pray!

I'm not suggesting that if you pray you'll never be sick again or never have an unpaid bill or never fail to see the will of God for your life. But I am saying there are many times when God will indeed heal you, times when He'll

provide for you, times when He'll reveal His will to you—
and the only thing that He's waiting for is for you to ask
_____ Him for that. And sometimes He will
ask you to wrestle in prayer for it.

You do not have because you do not ask.

Have you ever been in what
appeared to an impossible situation
with no way out? Have you ever desperately needed something, but there
seemed to be no way it could ever be
yours? Have you ever thought there
was no future for you, that it was just too late?

One thing that undeniably stands out in the pages of
Scripture is the fact that prayer can dramatically change
tough situations and tough people—and sometimes even
the course of nature:

Jehoshaphat, king of Judah, receives the sudden
report of a vast enemy army quickly approaching.
He immediately proclaims a nationwide fast and
leads his gathered people in prayer for deliverance,
concluding with these words to the Lord: "We
have no power against this great multitude that is
coming against us; nor do we know what to do,
but our eyes are upon You" (2 Chronicles 20:12).
The next day, Jehoshaphat leads his soldiers to the
place where God's prophet told them to go, and

there they find nothing but the dead bodies of their enemies.

A man named Elijah prays, and the rain in Israel stops for three and a half years. He prays again and the rain returns. He prays on another occasion, and fire comes down from heaven.

A woman named Hannah is unable to have a child. In heartbroken tearfulness she prays and pours out her soul to God. Soon Hannah conceives, and the son she gives birth to, Samuel, one day becomes one of Israel's greatest prophets.

As a blinded captive of the Philistines, Samson prays, and despite his previous disobedience, God gives him back his superhuman strength to effect one last defeat of his enemies.

The apostle James is arrested and executed; it's Peter's turn next. But his fellow believers employ a secret weapon: "constant prayer" (Acts 12:5). This word for "constant" literally means "stretched outwardly," or even "with agony"; it speaks of souls stretched out in earnest desire. (The same word is used of Jesus in Luke 22:44—"He prayed more earnestly. And His sweat became like great drops of blood falling down to the ground.") The church storms the gates of heaven, praying passionately and fervently for Peter's deliverance. And on the night before Peter's trial, an angel leads him out of prison, and Peter is soon out preaching the gospel again.

Paul and Silas are chained in a prison. At midnight they're praying and singing hymns. God sends an earthquake that tears off their chains and throws open the prison doors.

We read these accounts and we can't relate to them. After all, those were Bible heroes, the superspiritual. But what does Scripture tell us of Elijah? "Elijah was *a man with a nature like ours,* and he prayed earnestly that it would not rain; and it did not rain on the land for three years and six months. And he prayed again, and the heaven gave rain" (James 5:17–18).

OVERCOMING WORRY
We should also pray because prayer is the way God helps us overcome anxiety. Maybe you're struggling with a load of worry right now. Then the Bible's message right now for you is "Be anxious for nothing." And what does it say next?

Pray about whatever is significant? Or pray about the really huge concerns? No, what's next is this: "But *in everything* by prayer and supplication, with thanksgiving, let your requests be made known to God" (Philippians 4:6).

Worry about *nothing;* pray about *everything.* You can't really do the first without the second.

And when we do finally pray instead of worry, God replaces our anxiety with something priceless—His very own peace!

> Tell God what you need, and thank him for all he has done. If you do this, you will experience God's peace, which is far more wonderful than the human mind can understand. His peace will guard your hearts and minds as you live in Christ Jesus. (Philippians 4:6–7, NLT)

Are you having trouble sleeping at night because of the worries on your mind? I don't want to sound too mystical, but you can almost *feel* the calming effect of prayers expressing trust in God. This kind of prayer has a way of reminding us of the promises of God's Word, like these words from David: "I will both lie down in peace, and sleep; for You alone, O LORD, make me dwell in safety" (Psalm 4:8). Our sleeping-pill and tranquilizer-saturated society could certainly take a lesson from David on that one!

Your burden may seem insignificant, but you can bring it before the Lord without any embarrassment.

There's absolutely *nothing* you're tempted to worry about that you won't be better off talking to God about instead. God sees every detail in your life, and He cares about it all—even when other people don't understand.

David knew this. He told the Lord, "You keep track of all my sorrows. You have collected all my tears in your bottle. You have recorded each one in your book. On the very day I call to you for help, my enemies will retreat. This I know: God is on my side" (Psalm 56:8–9, NLT).

Your burden may seem insignificant to someone else, but you can bring it before the Lord without any embarrassment. He keeps your tears in a bottle. They are written in His book. That's the degree of personal compassion He has for each and every one of us.

Don't wait for a small thing to become a big thing. Bring the small thing before the Lord right now and pray about it. Your heavenly Father is interested in every facet of your life; don't reduce the infinite to the finite by placing limits on Him.

WHEN THE ANSWERS DON'T COME

Have you ever wondered why sometimes your prayers *aren't* answered?

In one important sense, all our prayers really *are* answered. Instead of answering "Yes," God in His wise love for us sometimes says to us "No" or "Wait."

As I look back, I'm glad God didn't say yes to every prayer I've prayed. I realize now that if the Lord had allowed what I prayed for, it might have harmed me. It could have been too much too soon, and I wasn't ready to handle it.

But at the same time, none of us like to hear "No." And hearing "Wait" doesn't suit us much better. We might respond, "God didn't answer my prayer," but what we really mean is "I don't like God's answer."

Another way to think of it is that sometimes God answers "Go," and sometimes He tells us "Slow." And then there are times when He turns down our request, and He's saying "Grow!" He wants us to do some spiritual maturing first.

"Grow" was essentially how God answered the apostle Paul when he prayed three times for his "thorn in the flesh" to be removed. God used that occasion to teach Paul (and us) this truth: "My grace is sufficient for you, for My strength is made perfect in weakness" (2 Corinthians 12:9).

But have you ever prayed with all your heart for something that you were convinced was the will of God and received nothing in response but an icy silence from heaven? Perhaps you were praying for the salvation of a loved one. Maybe it was a prayer asking God to send revival in your church, community, or nation.

You know in your innermost being that what you're praying for is pleasing and acceptable to God. So why doesn't He answer?

It's hard when we don't hear from God. We think, *What's going on? Is God paying attention? Is God concerned? Has He forgotten about me?*

We'll start to find answers as we truly grasp what happened one day when a desperate mother came to Jesus.

Chapter Three

A MOTHER
WHO WOULDN'T
GIVE UP

In Matthew 15, we find a reminder that those things we think are barriers from God are often, in reality, bridges to His greater blessings. The story told is that of a mother who wouldn't quit asking Jesus to heal her daughter, and it's a story that gives hope to all parents who care about the well-being of their children. It also gives us a different and fascinating perspective on wrestling with the Lord.

As the story begins, Jesus initially puts this woman off, as though He just doesn't have time for a non-Jew coming to Him for help. But another dynamic is at work. He isn't trying to destroy her faith; He is developing it. He isn't trying to make the situation more difficult; He is drawing her faith out. He knows she will overcome any barriers in her path because her faith is strong, and He wants to commend her.

We're told that this woman is a Canaanite, which means she probably is a worshiper of pagan deities. She may have become disillusioned with these false gods, because she comes seeking Jesus, the one true God. She has an accurate assessment of her own spiritual condition when she comes; she doesn't demand anything from the Lord, but instead cries for mercy, saying, "Have mercy on me, O Lord, Son of David! My daughter is severely demon-possessed" (Matthew 15:22).

This mother, like any good mother, cares desperately about the condition of her daughter, who has come under the power of demonic spirits. How the daughter ended up this way, we don't know. Perhaps her mother's pagan involvement up to that point has affected her daughter. Maybe there are many little idols and gods in the home, and these have opened a doorway to demonic power in this girl's life.

This is a reminder that actions and beliefs do have a direct influence on our children. We see it all too often in our society as crimes and sins are passed from generation to generation. For instance, statistics show that children of divorced parents are far more likely to end up divorcing as well. And children whose parents struggle with alcoholism and other addictions are likely to struggle with these issues, too. Only the power of God can break these cycles of sin.

A SERIES OF BARRIERS

This mother comes to Jesus with her heartfelt need, casting herself on His mercy. Jesus' reaction might lead us to believe that He was heartless and uncaring. But nothing could be further from the truth. What is in fact happening is that Jesus is testing the faith of this woman by setting up a series of barriers.

First, He is silent: "He answered her not a word" (v. 23). Sometimes the hardest response to accept is no response at all. But what appears to be a brush-off is actually an invitation for her to step in, to be persistent and not let go.

The disciples, however, interpret their Master's silence to mean He doesn't want to be bothered, especially since the woman is creating a bit of a scene. His disciples urge Him, saying, "Send her away, for she cries out after us" (v. 23).

"Lord," they say, "get rid of this nagging lady." Jesus doesn't throw her out, but the way He responds doesn't exactly sound like an invitation for her to stick around either: "I was not sent except to the lost sheep of the house of Israel" (v. 24).

Slam! The door is shut in this mother's face. But she

just keeps knocking. She refuses to be discouraged in her quest.

So she comes and worships Him, saying, "Lord, help me!" (v. 25).

But Jesus isn't through testing her perseverance. He answers, "It is not good to take the children's bread and throw it to the little dogs" (v. 26).

Dogs? Not exactly a compliment. Maybe now this woman will give up her hopeless quest! But when Christ calls her a dog, she just picks up what He says and brings it back to Him—like a faithful hound picking up the master's stick and dropping it at his feet.

She says, "True, Lord, yet even the little dogs eat the crumbs which fall from their masters' table" (v. 27).

I think a smile crosses the face of Jesus at that moment. The woman's faith is so great that she knows even a tiny leftover of Jesus' power will be enough to heal her daughter.

Jesus has heard what He wanted to hear. Now He dramatically changes His manner with her. He says, "O woman, great is your faith! Let it be to you as you desire" (v. 28).

The mouths of the disciples drop open at this. All this time they thought Jesus was brushing her off, clearly stamping her request with a *no*. Then suddenly He turns around and tells the Canaanite woman essentially that she can have whatever she wants! He is giving her carte blanche. What a statement! *"Let it be... as you desire."*

What she desires, of course, is her daughter's freedom from a devilish influence in her life—and she gets it. In fact, her daughter is healed "that very hour" (v. 28).

So what qualified this woman to have such a thing said to her? What brought her to a place where Jesus would offer her such an incredible privilege?

Above all, I think it had to be her persistence, her tenacity, her commitment. This is the kind of faith *we* need. When we're praying for something we believe is in accordance with the will of God, we should not give up. If at first you don't succeed, keep asking, keep seeking, and keep knocking.

PASSIONATE AND PERSISTENT

Remember the story Jesus told of the friend who came at midnight to pound on his neighbor's door and ask for bread? It was late, and the man and his family were asleep, for crying out loud! This was no time for getting up to gather a few loaves of bread. But Jesus makes this point:

> I say to you, though he will not rise and give to him because he is his friend, yet *because of his persistence* he will rise and give him as many as he needs. (Luke 11:8)

Then our Lord tells us, "And I say to you, ask, and it will be given to you; seek, and you will find; knock, and it will be opened to you. For everyone who asks receives, and he who seeks finds, and to him who knocks it will be opened" (11:9–10).

Often in prayer we will ask God for something once or twice, then give up. But God doesn't want us to take His silence for a final answer; instead we are to ask, seek, and knock.

Jesus' language in this verse is unusually compelling, because these three verbs indicate an ascending order of intensity.

"Ask" implies our request for assistance. We realize our need and ask for help. The word also implies that we are to be humble in submitting our request.

"Seek" also denotes asking but adds the aspect of *action*. We don't just express our need, but we get up and look around for help. This involves effort—the prayerful effort of searching for God's answers, especially in His Word!

God doesn't want us to take His silence for a final answer.

"Knock" includes asking, taking action, *and* the aspect of persevering—like the neighbor pounding on his friend's door at midnight.

So the stacking of these words is extremely forceful, as is the Greek verb tense used. The literal meaning is this: *"Keep on asking and it will be given to you; keep on seeking and you will find it; keep on knocking and the door will be opened."*

Jesus is calling us to passionate, persistent prayer!

STALKING THE JUDGE

When Jesus said that we "always ought to pray and not lose heart," He told another vivid story to get across that concept to His disciples.

> There was in a certain city a judge who did not fear God nor regard man. Now there was a widow in that city; and she came to him, saying, "Avenge me of my adversary." (Luke 18:2–3)

This judge would likely be one of the men appointed to such positions by the Romans or by King Herod—men who were notorious for their corruption.

The person bringing a plea before this judge was first of all a woman, meaning she had little standing in the culture of that time. Moreover, she was a widow, having no husband to be her advocate in court. With no husband, she was also probably poor, with no money to offer the judge a bribe. She had nothing to fall back on except persistence with a capital *P.*

At first the judge paid her no attention, but then he gets to thinking.

> But afterward he said within himself, "Though I do not fear God nor regard man, yet because this widow troubles me I will avenge her, lest by her continual coming she weary me." (vv. 4–5)

In other words, this woman was driving him crazy. The Greek word used here for the verb *trouble* is very suggestive—the image it gives is of beating someone black and blue or giving them a black eye. Essentially this judge was thinking, *If I don't give this woman what she wants, she's going to beat me senseless!* It almost sounds as if she was stalking the judge. No wonder he decided to give her what she wanted.

So what's the point? Should we threaten God? Do we need to bully Him to get Him to do what we want?

Look at the lesson Jesus teaches:

> And shall God not avenge His own elect who cry out day and night to Him, though He bears long with them? I tell you that He will avenge them speedily. Nevertheless, when the Son of Man comes, will He really find faith on the earth? (vv. 6–8)

If a poor widow got what she deserved from a selfish judge, how much more will God's children receive what is right from their loving heavenly Father!

Think with me now about the differences between the widow's situation and our own:

1. This woman was a stranger to the judge, but we come before God as His children.

2. This widow had no guaranteed access to the judge, but God's children have open access to him 24–7. At any time, "we can boldly enter heaven's Most Holy Place because of the blood of Jesus" (Hebrews 10:19, NLT). "Let us therefore come boldly to the throne of grace, that we may obtain mercy and find grace to help in time of need" (Hebrews 4:16).

3. This woman had no friend at court to plead her case, no husband or attorney to stand up and defend her— no inside connection at all. All she could do was walk around the outside of the judge's quarters and shout threats! By contrast, "we have an Advocate with the Father, Jesus Christ the righteous" (1 John 2:1). We *always* have an attorney before God—and He's the Son of the Judge!

Not only that, but we also have the Holy Spirit teaching us how to pray and taking hold of us in our prayers— energizing and directing our prayers—so that they're delivered through Jesus Christ before a loving heavenly Father who so eagerly wants to answer us and bless us!

That's why the Lord wants us to keep on praying and not lose heart.

WHATEVER YOU WANT

Remember how Jesus at last responded to that Canaanite woman with the stricken daughter? What would it take for God to come to you right now and say, "I will give you whatever you want, no limits—you name it and it's yours"? Have you shown the kind of full-of-faith perseverance that He wants to reward like that?

Your children can escape your presence, but they cannot escape your prayers.

Maybe you, like this woman, know what it's like to have a child who's under the devil's influence. He or she has rejected your influence and God's influence, at least for now. Don't give up, and don't feel like the Lord has abandoned you or failed you. Keep praying. Your children can escape your presence, but they cannot escape your prayers.

As you pray, make it your goal to find out the will of God and pray accordingly. Prayer isn't getting your way in heaven; it's getting God's way on earth.

What do you really want today? Salvation for your

child? for your husband? for your friend? Then don't give up praying for each of them.

Or maybe it's not your child in trouble, but you. You've reached rock bottom yourself. Don't be embarrassed to come to the Lord with your problems and ask for His assistance. Call out to Him. Don't be discouraged. He's ready to help you and forgive you, and to start changing you.

Don't let the devil whisper into your ear that it's too late—or worse, that God doesn't care. Remember that what may look like indifference on God's part may actually be a barrier that He wants you to overcome by persistent, faithful wrestling in prayer.

Keep praying!

The prayer that has "wrestling" power with God is the one that is offered continually and earnestly. The prayer that prevails with Him is the one that we put our whole soul into, stretching out toward Him in intense and agonizing desire.

For God long ago promised that His people will find Him when they search for Him with all their heart (see Jeremiah 29:13).

Chapter Four

GET ALIGNED WITH GOD'S WILL

Jesus once gave this incredible promise on how to experience answered prayer: "If you abide in Me, and My words abide in you, you will ask what you desire, and it shall be done for you" (John 15:7). This promise could also be translated, "If you maintain a living communion with Me, and My Word is at home with you, I command you to ask at once for whatever your heart desires, and it will be yours."

When I read this passage, I immediately gravitate toward the promise at the end of it. If I ask for whatever my heart desires, it's mine. But then I read more closely what Jesus said before that—a condition to be met: "If you maintain a living communion with Me, and My Word is at home with you...."

WANTING WHAT GOD WANTS

To abide like this speaks of intimacy, closeness, and friendship. It's the picture of two friends who are comfortable in each other's presence. You aren't ill at ease with each other, looking forward to getting away. You enjoy being together, and you want to hear what each other has to say.

Of course, this must be balanced with a healthy reverence and awe of who God is. We aren't to become overly casual with Him—He's the Almighty God and He's to be revered, worshiped, and obeyed. But He's also our Father in heaven who greatly desires to hear from us and wants to be our closest and most intimate friend.

Likewise when Jesus says we must let His words abide in us, it means letting the Scriptures be at home in our heart. Therefore our prayers cannot be divorced from our lifestyles. They flow out of a close walk with God. If our life isn't pleasing to God, effective prayer life will be practically nonexistent.

If that's what is happening in our lives—living in communion with the Lord and staying at home in His Word— then we're going to want what *He* wants. He'll be changing our outlook, our desires, and eventually our prayers. If we abide in Jesus, we'll grow to the point of being able to "automatically" sense God's will, and so we'll be asking for it in prayer.

HIS LISTENING EAR

So the prayer that prevails with God involves something more than sheer gut-it-out persistence. Persevering prayer that's truly effective will always keep bringing us more closely aligned with God's will as we find ourselves wanting more and more what He wants.

The primary objective of wrestling prayer is to line our will up with the will of God. Only when we do that will we see more of our prayers answered in the affirmative. Nothing lies outside the reach of prayer—except what lies outside the will of God. God answers only the requests which He Himself inspires.

Nothing lies outside the reach of prayer— except what lies outside the will of God.

True wrestling prayer is not getting God to move your way; it's getting you to move His way. It's not bending God to my perspective and attitude, but bending myself to His. It doesn't even involve "informing" God of anything, for Jesus told us, "Your Father knows the things you have need of before you ask Him" (Matthew 6:8).

As Martin Luther said, "By our praying we are instructing ourselves more than Him."

Why does God answer our prayers? "[We] receive from

him anything we ask *because we obey his commands and do what pleases him"* (1 John 3:22, NIV).

If you give a listening ear to all of God's commands, He'll give a listening ear to all your prayers to Him. If you'll agree with Him, He'll agree with you; if you don't yield to Him, He won't yield to you.

Charles Spurgeon said, "When you have great desires for heavenly things, when your desires are such as God approves of, when you want what God wants, then you will have what you like." That's the key—when your desires are such as God approves of. Get your will in alignment with His.

How do you do it? Spend time in God's presence. Be at home in His Word. Study the Bible; get it into your blood; know it well. Apply what you read there, and let God change your outlook.

A BLANK CHECK FROM GOD

Coming back again to the Canaanite woman with the demon-possessed daughter, remember how Jesus eventually said to her, "Let it be to you as you desire" (Matthew 15:28)? God doesn't offer a blank check like that to just anyone. If we're thinking only of ourselves or are motivated by greed, we need not apply. But to the humble person who isn't questioning God's will but is rather surrendering to it, God offers such a possibility.

If you had a blank check from God, what would you tell Him you really want?

Is it the salvation of your child, your husband or wife, a friend, or even your enemy? Maybe it has seemed that the more you pray for them, the farther away from God they get. They may be antagonistic, argumentative, hardened against anything you say. You wonder if your prayers are doing any good.

But don't give up. Keep asking, seeking, knocking. You just don't know how much God is already at work. Maybe He's taking them "all the way down" so they'll get the picture and ask for His help up. Maybe their antagonism is actually the result of the Holy Spirit's conviction in their life. We just don't know.

> *If you had a blank check from God, what would you tell Him you really want?*

Do you really want to see a spiritual awakening sweep America? Persist in prayer. We can't begin to imagine how much God will do in answer to such pleading.

Remember that there are certain things Satan doesn't want you to pray for. In one sense, he doesn't want you to pray for anything. But there are some things he *really* doesn't want you to pray for.

Satan doesn't want us to pray for revival in America, because he knows that's the only thing that could turn our people back to God and bring about any lasting moral change. And I doubt Satan wants you to pray for the salvation of any unbelievers you know.

Concerning issues like that, there may be spiritual warfare happening behind the scenes that goes far beyond our capacity to understand. At a time of great spiritual wrestling in Daniel's life, an angel appeared and told the prophet that his prayers had been heard from the first but that the angel had been delayed in coming to him for three weeks because of a struggle with demonic forces that required the help of the archangel Michael (see Daniel 10:12–13). This amazing account is a reminder that God's delays are not necessarily His denials. Those are the times when God is building up our faith.

Never forget that what may look like God's insensitivity is nothing of the sort, but rather an invitation to draw closer to Him through persistent praying in faith.

COME RULE AND REIGN

One day, Jesus was praying, and when He finished, one of the disciples made a beautiful request: "Lord, teach us to pray" (Luke 11:1).

Jesus answered by giving them the model prayer—not merely a prayer to pray, but rather a guide for all prayer, a pattern to follow. Without question it's a powerful prayer, and there's certainly nothing wrong with praying it verbatim.

But it's even more helpful as a pattern to keep in mind as we approach God, especially when engaging in wrestling prayer. When we're feeling called to really "get down to business" with God, that's probably the most important time to remember the nuts and bolts that Jesus says are essential to the process of prayer.

Now, if Jesus had asked *me* to write that model prayer instead of teaching it to us Himself, it might start this way: "Our Father who art in heaven, give us our daily bread." You know, cut to the chase. Let's get down to business. "How are You, Lord? Nice to be with You. *Now here's what I need....*"

That's how we often pray, rushing into God's presence and rattling off our grocery list. So to be honest, maybe we really ought to be saying, "Our Santa who art in heaven..." or "Our vending machine who art in heaven...."

But according to the pattern Jesus gave us, before we utter a single word of personal petition, we should pray for God's kingdom to come and for His will to be done. Only then do we ask Him to give us this day our daily bread.

"Your kingdom come"—that's what Jesus told us to pray (v. 2). This is a multilevel request with different shades of meaning. It's first of all a request for the return of Jesus to this earth. The word Jesus uses here for "kingdom" doesn't primarily refer to a geographical territory, but rather to sovereignty and dominion. When we pray, "Your kingdom come," we're praying for God's rule on earth, which essentially begins when Jesus returns to rule and reign. It's the request reflected in the Bible's closing prayer: "Even so, come, Lord Jesus!" (Revelation 22:20).

And the word translated as "come" indicates a sudden, instantaneous coming. I'm praying "Lord, please come back and do it soon!" Is your life right now in such a spiritual condition that you can pray this? The answer to that question is a real indicator of where you are with God.

Is your expectation of the Lord's return alive and well? The Bible says that "everyone who has this hope in Him purifies himself, just as He is pure" (1 John 3:3). The person who is seeking to know God and is walking in holiness with Him has every reason to long for His return.

His Kingdom for Me

The prayer "Your kingdom come" is also a personal request. With that prayer, I'm asking for the kingdom of God to come in my own life. "For indeed," Jesus said, "the kingdom of God is within you" (Luke 17:21). He was referring to His own presence on that particular day. The kingdom of God speaks of the present rule and reign of Jesus Christ.

With this prayer I'm saying, "Lord, I want Your rule

and reign in my life. I want to live by Your principles found in Your Word. I want You to be in charge. I give You the master key to every room in my life."

But know this: We can't pray "Your kingdom come" until we pray "My kingdom go." So when Jesus says, "Seek first the kingdom of God and His righteousness" (Matthew 6:33), He's saying, "In everything you say and do, before anything else, seek first and foremost the rule and reign of God in your life."

So when I pray "Your kingdom come, Your will be done," I'm saying, "Lord, if the personal requests I'm about to ask for are in any way outside of Your will, overrule them!"

His Kingdom for Others

The prayer "Your kingdom come" is also an evangelistic prayer. It's a request for the salvation of those who don't know the Lord. As His kingdom is ruling and reigning in our own lives, we can have a part in bringing it to others as we pray to that end.

There's no doubt that the will of God includes people coming to believe in Jesus Christ. God is "not willing that any should perish but that all should come to repentance" (2 Peter 3:9).

Jesus Himself modeled this kind of praying for us. Isaiah's messianic prophecy tells us that Christ "made intercession for the transgressors" (Isaiah 53:12). On the cross, Jesus prayed, "Father, forgive them, for they do not know what they do" (Luke 23:34).

A striking example of prayer for nonbelievers is shown in the case of Stephen in Acts. As he was being stoned for his bold, uncompromising stand for Jesus, "he knelt down and cried out with a loud voice, 'Lord, do not charge them with this sin.' And when he had said this, he fell asleep" (Acts 7:60).

We know that a young man named Saul of Tarsus was watching all this happen that day. Could it be that Stephen, inspired by the Holy Spirit, might have been praying especially for Saul? Later, when Saul was converted, it was so unexpected that many of the Christians didn't believe it. Do you know someone right now whom you cannot even imagine becoming a Christian? Start praying for that person! No one is beyond the reach of prayer or the need of salvation.

Paul himself spoke of the prayer burden he had for the Jews to come to Jesus: "My heart's desire and prayer to God for Israel is that they may be saved" (Romans 10:1).

Though it isn't biblical to "claim" someone's salvation—only God knows if and when that person will truly believe—it is *very* biblical for us to pray, and pray a lot, for unbelievers to come to Christ.

His Will Be Done

In the model prayer that Jesus gave us, the request "Your kingdom come" is joined with this one: *"Your will be done* on earth as it is in heaven."

This request, too, has a personal aspect to it: "Your will be done in my life, just as it is in heaven."

This request also includes a prayer concern for others, believers and unbelievers alike: "Your will be done in *his* life and in *her* life, just as it is in heaven."

When it comes to our willingness to let God's will be done, the story of Jacob's wrestling with God is full of helpful instruction. As I promised earlier, it's time take a closer look at that amazing incident.

Chapter Five

WHEN THE LORD
BECAME A
WRESTLER

The story of Jacob is the story of a man who wanted the will of God for his life but had an annoying habit of trying to give God "a little assistance." As we touched on before, Jacob clearly had a heart for God but at the same time displayed a tendency to be dishonest and scheming.

Jacob always thought he was on God's side, but one day he discovered he'd actually been on his own side—instead of fighting *for* God, he ended up fighting *with* God. Up to this point he had been using God instead of allowing God to use him.

AN ORDINARY GUY

In many ways, Jacob was pretty ordinary, someone not much different from you or me. He wasn't a man of great bravery like Daniel or like Shadrach, Meshach, and Abednego. Jacob, in fact, was a bit on the cowardly side.

Jacob wasn't really noted for his great faith like his grandfather Abraham. Nor was he a man of great integrity like his son Joseph, but rather, he was often calculating and wily. You'll recall that at his birth he was given the name Jacob, which meant "heel catcher, contender, supplanter." This pretty much summed up his life thereafter.

The pattern was already established when—as a single young man leaving home because of a threat from his brother Esau, whom he had cheated—Jacob received from God a vision of angels going up and down a ladder to heaven, while at the top of it, God Himself stood and announced a promise to bless Jacob and his descendants and to be with him wherever he went. You would think this experience would change Jacob forever—no more deception, no more helping God out. But an "experience with God"—no matter how awesome—doesn't guarantee we

An "experience with God"—no matter how awesome—doesn't guarantee we will never fall into sin.

will never fall into sin. After Jacob departed Canaan and came to the land of Haran, his deception and trickery were soon evident once again.

Finally, many years later, after Jacob had acquired a huge family and vast wealth in the form of livestock, God told him to return to Canaan. It was time for Jacob to face his past and the wrongs he'd committed. It was time to deal with Esau.

Jacob couldn't retreat from this encounter; he had nowhere to go but forward. And waiting for him was Esau, the brother he had cheated out of his birthright some twenty years earlier.

The Lord knew the fear that was in Jacob's heart, so He came to him in a special way.

With Angels, Yet Afraid

Genesis 32 records Jacob's encounter with God that marks the turning point in this man's life.

> So Jacob went on his way, and the angels of God met him. When Jacob saw them, he said, "This is God's camp." And he called the name of that place Mahanaim. (Genesis 32:1–2)

That word "Mahanaim" means "two camps," and this word for "camp" means "host" or "army." Jacob was acknowledging that in this place was not only his camp, but also God's camp. The Lord was saying to him, "You're not alone, Jacob. There's no reason to be afraid!"

What was Jacob's need in this hour? Protection. So God sent an entire camp of angels to reassure him.

God's provision comes to us exactly when it's needed. He's never too soon or too late! God anticipates our need and provides His grace just when we need it. Whatever the circumstances or emergency, He'll be there. "For He Himself has said, 'I will never leave you nor forsake you'" (Hebrews 13:5).

But then came word from Jacob's advance scouts that Esau was up ahead, waiting with four hundred men to meet him. "So Jacob was greatly afraid and distressed" (Genesis 32:7).

Here was an army of angels camped beside him, yet Jacob is afraid and immediately begins to plot and scheme his way forward. He decides to split his family and livestock into two camps, telling himself, "If Esau comes to the one company and attacks it, then the other company which is left will escape" (v. 8).

After Jacob implemented these plans, he then asked God to bless them. Like so many of us, he seemed to believe that "God helps those who help themselves" —a statement that not only isn't found in the Bible, but isn't scriptural in its content. Neither was it true for Jacob.

Notice what Jacob then prays:

O God of my father Abraham and God of my father Isaac, the LORD who said to me, "Return to your country and to your kindred, and I will deal well with you": I am not worthy of the least of all the mercies and of all the truth which You have shown Your servant; for I crossed over this Jordan with my staff, and now I have become two companies. *Deliver me, I pray, from the hand of my brother,* from the hand of Esau; for I fear him, lest he come and attack me and the mother with the children. (vv. 9–11)

This, by the way, is the first recorded prayer we have coming from Jacob, though at this point his story has already taken up seven chapters of Genesis. It causes you to wonder whether Jacob had ever done any praying before. Maybe it was his lack of prayer—and thus his lack of dependence upon God—that caused him to always feel he had to "make it all happen" himself.

And yet there are a number of positive aspects to his prayer, a prayer that God both heard and answered. Jacob first acknowledged the God of his grandfather Abraham and his father, Isaac, as the one true God. And he confessed his own unworthiness before bringing his petition to the Lord.

Nevertheless, even as he was praying, Jacob probably

was plotting his next step. As soon as the prayer was done, he went to work on his own plan again, sending successive droves of livestock ahead as an appeasement to Esau. Jacob was leaving nothing to chance!

Night came after he and his family had reached the brook of Jabbok. Jacob helped his family to ford this stream, then lingered back on the other side.

And there it happened—the encounter with God that would forever change his life.

GOD THE WRESTLER

Everything Jacob owned was now stretched out ahead of him across the desert. At the very back, last of all, was Jacob himself.

Now it was time for the Lord Himself to make an appearance to Jacob, since an army of angels obviously wasn't enough. It's a reminder that God meets us at whatever level He finds us in order to lift us to where He wants us to be. To Abraham the pilgrim, God came as a traveler (see Genesis 18). Centuries later, on the eve of the battle of Jericho, He appeared "as Commander of the army of the LORD" to Joshua the general (Joshua 5:14).

And now to Jacob, a man who'd spent most of his life wrestling with people, figuratively speaking, God came as a wrestler. As David would acknowledge before God centuries later, "With the pure You will show Yourself pure; and with the devious You will show Yourself shrewd" (Psalm 18:26).

Let's look closely at Jacob's amazing encounter:

Then Jacob was left alone; and a Man wrestled with him until the breaking of day. Now when He saw that He did not prevail against him, He touched the socket of his hip; and the socket of Jacob's hip was out of joint as He wrestled with him. And He said, "Let Me go, for the day breaks."

But he said, "I will not let You go unless You bless me!"

So He said to him, "What is your name?"

And he said, "Jacob."

And He said, "Your name shall no longer be called Jacob, but Israel; for you have struggled with God and with men, and have prevailed."

Then Jacob asked Him, saying, "Tell me Your name, I pray."

And He said, "Why is it that you ask about My name?" And He blessed him there.

And Jacob called the name of the place Peniel: "For I have seen God face to face, and my life is preserved." (Genesis 32:24–30)

Remember again that this was no mere angel, but the Lord Himself whom Jacob was wrestling with. Jacob called the place Peniel, which means "I have seen God face to face."

And note that this encounter happened only when Jacob was "left alone." C. H. Mackintosh writes:

> To be left alone with God is the only true way of arriving at a just knowledge of ourselves and our ways.... No matter what we may think about ourselves, nor yet what man may think about us, the great question is, what does God think about us?

When we get away from all the distractions, alone with God, we can get an unbiased and correct judgment of ourselves. Why are we so often afraid to do this?

Instead we clutter our lives with activities, like busy Martha, rather than sit at Jesus' feet like Mary. Have you truly been alone with God lately?

LET ME CHANGE YOU

Once the Lord had Jacob there alone, He asked him a significant question: "What is your name?"

Why that question? Because to answer it honestly, Jacob had to make an admission. Remember the meaning of Jacob's name. In essence, the Lord was asking him, "Are you going to continue living up to your name, deceiving others? Or will you admit what you are and let me change you?"

This was a question only Jacob could answer.

It's a question God asks each of us as well: "Do you want to stay as you have been? Or will you let Me transform your life?"

There was once a man in Jerusalem who had been an invalid for thirty-eight years—a terribly long time. Day after day he waited by a little pool of water called Bethesda where angelic healings sometimes occurred. Jesus saw the man lying there and said to him, "Do you want to be made well?"

Now why would Jesus ask such a question? Wasn't the answer obvious?

Not necessarily. As strange as it may seem, there many people today do not want help. They like the lifestyle they've chosen, even though it causes them so much harm. They find a certain comfort in the darkness; they feel a sense of security there. It's home to them, like a sty to a pig.

> "Do you want to stay as you have been? Or will you let Me transform your life?"

Years ago our youngest son, Jonathan, had a little pet rat that he named Grommet. Jonathan's older brother, Christopher, thought it might be a good idea to build

Grommet a little house out of Popsicle sticks to fit inside the cage.

When the house was done, it was adorable. It even had little windows and a front door that Grommet could walk through. The boys set the new house inside the cage, and we all looked on as the little rat inspected his new quarters and seemed to like it.

But the next morning, when we came to see how Grommet was doing in his new digs, we were shocked to find that he had eaten it.

You see, a rat is always a rat, and rats don't live in cute little houses! They prefer sewers and cellars and other dark and dirty places. And they don't really want to change.

That's the way it is with many people. They become so hardened in their sin that they prefer the dark ways of death and emptiness. "Sin enough," says Oswald Chambers, "and you will soon be unconscious of sin."

But we don't have to stay in our sin. God always offers us the way out. He won't force His will or way in our lives. But He asks us, "Are you willing to give Me control?"

We can hear the same question when Jesus says, "Take My yoke upon you and learn from Me" (Matthew 11:29). A yoke is a steering device. Jesus is saying, "Let Me steer and guide your life! Will you let Me do that?"

I don't know about you, but I'm one of the world's worst backseat drivers. On those rare occasions when my wife is driving and I'm the passenger, such as when she picks me up at the airport, I'm constantly advising her: "Cathe, there's a light up there; slow down. You need to get in your left lane—our turn is coming up...."

We can be like this with the Lord, too: "Lord, you better do this right now," or "I don't really think that's a good idea there, God," and so on.

Have you seen the bumper sticker that says "God Is My Copilot"? I hate to break this to you, but God *doesn't want* to be your copilot. He doesn't even want you in the cockpit! Jesus wants only *His* hands on the steering wheel of our lives. He doesn't want or need us to be backseat drivers or copilots.

TEARFUL SURRENDER

Why did God wrestle with Jacob? To bring him to the point of surrender, reducing him to a sense of his nothingness and causing him to see what a poor, helpless, weak person he really was—and that in such weakness lay his true strength.

For this same reason, the Lord instructed Gideon to shrink his army before going into battle (see Judges 7). It's the same reason He told the great Syrian commander Naaman to strip his clothes and dunk himself seven times in the muddy Jordan River to be healed of his leprosy (see 2 Kings 5). For the same reason, God often went out of His way to find obscure instruments to work through, like the sheepherder David or the coarse fisherman Peter.

"My grace is sufficient for you," God said to Paul, "for My strength is made perfect in weakness" (2 Corinthians 12:9). Or literally, "My grace is enough for you, for power is moment by moment coming to its full energy and complete operation in the sphere of weakness."

Maybe that's even happening to you right now, and that's why it seems that you must wrestle with God—when it's really your own will you're wrestling with! If so, remember that God's plan and purpose for your life are far better than any you may have dreamed or plotted for yourself.

Jacob surrendered to God. "He wept, and sought favor from Him" (Hosea 12:4). Instead of fighting with the Lord, he asked in tears for His blessing. God brought him from cunning to clinging, from resisting to resting. Jacob had now been brought to the end of his resources, painful though it was.

Instead of fighting with the Lord, Jacob asked in tears for His blessing.

And having surrendered, Jacob was given a new name—Israel. Scholars differ on what this name means. Some of the various interpretations are: one whom God commands, let God rule, one who fights victoriously with God, a prince with God, and God's fighter.

Whatever the name means, it's clear that a complete surrender took place in Jacob's life—a capitulation to God and His will for him. God was saying, "You're no longer the 'heel catcher' or 'supplanter.' Instead, you're someone marked by Me and named by Me. A prince with Me, a fighter with Me."

Jacob's loss in this wrestling match was also Jacob's victory! He won by losing and then was able to go forward in new strength as he walked in God's strength, in God's will, and in God's timing.

This is precisely what Jesus meant when He said, "For whoever desires to save his life will lose it, and whoever loses his life for My sake will find it" (Matthew 16:25).

When this wrestling match was over, Jacob said, "I have seen God face to face." The face of God always changes Jacobs to Israels, grabbers to receivers. It changes you and me as well. "We all, with unveiled face, beholding as in a mirror the glory of the Lord, *are being transformed* into the same image from glory to glory, just as by the Spirit of the Lord" (2 Corinthians 3:18). When we've spent time alone with God and seen His face, it will always transform and prepare us for what is yet ahead.

Chapter Six

CHECK YOUR
ATTITUDE

After his wrestling match with God, Jacob marveled: "I have seen God face to face, and my life is preserved" (Genesis 32:30). Though Jacob had been a wrestling partner with the Lord Himself, he still was overwhelmed with God's awesome and majestic holiness. He couldn't begin to understand how a man could wrestle with such a God and not be slain outright.

Remember in the model prayer how Jesus taught us to pray, "Our Father in heaven, *hallowed be Your name*"? In this blueprint for all prayer, Jesus shows us that in our initial approach to our Father, we should first contemplate His holiness and majesty and glory.

Once you sincerely pray "Hallowed be Your name," it can't help but alter your attitude. And attitude has big-time importance in any prayer, especially wrestling prayer where so much is at stake. Attitude can make or unmake a prayer. You can pray with all the persistence in the world, but if your heart isn't right before God, your doggedness isn't going to matter. Attitude means everything in effective prayer, and your attitude is inseparable from your view of God.

So in prayer wrestling, your first move is to grapple with the greatness of God—to lay hold of it, grasp it, and seize it in your mind and heart.

BIGGER GOD, SMALLER PROBLEMS

This word "hallowed" means "set apart," just as you might have some special silverware you set apart to use only for special occasions. When we pray "Hallowed be Your name," we're saying, "Lord, set apart your name. You are awesome and glorious and wonderful beyond anyone and anything else."

Wait before making your requests. Just contemplate God. When you do, here's what happens: All of a sudden, your needs and problems start shrinking—not because they're actually getting smaller, but because you're realizing how big God is by comparison. The reason you were so stressed-out before is because you were thinking how big your problem was and you forgot how big God is. You weren't seeing things in true perspective.

The more we remember the bigness of God, the smaller our problems seem in comparison. Scripture asks, "Is anything too hard for the LORD?" (Genesis 18:14). Of course not.

Praying this way means that I set God apart as first in my life—above everything else, as Lord over all. Because if He isn't Lord *of* all, He isn't Lord *at* all.

One day, Jesus asked someone to follow Him, and that person responded, "Lord, *let me first* go and bury my father." Jesus wouldn't agree to those terms. Then someone else said to Him, "Lord, I will follow You, but *let me first* go and bid them farewell who are at my house." Once more, Jesus didn't approve (Luke 9:59–62). The problem with these people was that each one said, "Lord…*me first.*" That's an oxymoron, like "genuine imitation" or "freezer burn." You can't legitimately call Jesus "Lord" and at the same time say, "Me first."

The more we remember the bigness of God, the smaller our problems seem in comparison.

To say sincerely "Hallowed be Your name" means that in my life and character I want to set the Lord above all else. I therefore must ask myself this question in all my interests, activities, ambitions, and pursuits: Is this for God's glory?

Can I write "Hallowed be Your name" over it?

What about the career choices I make, the friends I choose to be with, the TV programs and movies I watch, the music I listen to? Can I write "Hallowed be Your name" over all of that?

If not, I have some adjustments to make in my life—immediately.

HEART POSTURE

The right attitude is more than just getting on your knees or flat on your face before God, although there's no doubt that doing that can sometimes help you be more aware of where you are as you come before our holy God. But there's more to it than posture.

I heard about three ministers who were debating the most helpful posture in prayer. As they were talking, a telephone repairman was working on the phone system in the background.

One minister said he felt the key was in the hands—he always held his hands together and pointed them upward as a form of symbolic worship, and that really helped him pray with more focus.

The second guy suggested that the most heartfelt prayer always happened when you were on your knees.

The third minister suggested that the other two both had it wrong—the only position worth its salt was to stretch out flat on your face. That *really* brought intensity to your prayers.

By this time the telephone repairman could no longer stay out of the conversation. He blurted out, "The most powerful prayer I ever made was while dangling upside down by my heels off the top of a forty-foot power pole."

Yes, that would probably work, too.

It's not our physical posture, but the posture of the heart that God is really concerned about. "For the LORD does not see as man sees; for man looks at the outward appearance, but the LORD looks at the heart" (1 Samuel 16:7). And our prayers are sure to reveal what our heart's posture really is.

TWO MEN PRAYING

Have you ever been watching a movie and felt certain you knew how it was going to turn out—which guy would get the girl or who was really the bad guy—but then the story took a twist and delivered a surprise ending?

That was the case with a parable Jesus told about two men praying. The story started this way: "Two men went up to the temple to pray, one a Pharisee and the other a tax collector" (Luke 18:10).

As Jesus spoke those words, I think His listeners immediately settled right away on who was the hero and who was the villain in this story. Given the cultural setting in which the story was being told, surely the Pharisee would turn out to be the good guy, and the tax collector would be the bad guy.

Now this is hard for us to understand today because we've loaded additional meaning into the word *Pharisee,* and we think of it generally in a negative light. But it was different in Jesus' time. The Pharisees were thought of as great men of honor, men who committed themselves to the study of Scripture and to following God and obeying His law to the best of their ability, far beyond what ordinary folks would do.

Meanwhile, people back then didn't like tax collectors any more than we like them now—and probably much less. In those times people were overtaxed like we are today, only it was worse because the tax collector would add his own fee onto what he was already collecting for Rome. Not only that, but he was somewhat of a traitor—a Jew working for the hated Romans, collecting taxes from fellow Jews for the benefit of the occupying foreigners.

So when Jesus began His story, it would be like our saying today, "A minister and a drug dealer went to church to pray." Or "Mother Teresa and Adolf Hitler went to church to pray." Or Billy Graham and Marilyn Manson. Hearing it that way, you immediately identify in your own mind the good guy and the bad guy, and you think, *God will certainly hear the prayer of Billy Graham over the prayer of Marilyn Manson.* And why would God do that? Is it because Billy

Graham is a great evangelist? No, it would be because Billy Graham comes to God the same way you and I do, through the blood of Jesus Christ. Billy Graham has the same access to God that you and I have.

Back to our story. Let's see how the "hero" prays:

The Pharisee stood and prayed thus with himself, "God, I thank You that I am not like other men—extortioners, unjust, adulterers, or even as this tax collector. I fast twice a week; I give tithes of all that I possess." (vv. 11–12)

Notice first of all those two little words that Jesus slips in—this guy was praying "with himself." A literal rendering of this would be, "he prayed *to* himself." Did you know it's possible to pray to yourself? If there's no regard of God in your prayer, you're essentially praying to yourself, and your prayers are going nowhere. Many people regularly say their prayers and yet never really pray, because their heart isn't right with God. That's what was happening with this Pharisee.

Many people regularly say their prayers and yet never really pray.

At this point, it's good to look back at why Jesus was telling this story: "He spoke this parable to some *who trusted in themselves* that they were righteous, and despised others" (v. 9). This was the Pharisee's root problem—trusting in himself.

But let's not misunderstand. Jesus didn't criticize the Pharisee for fasting twice a week and giving away 10 percent of everything he owned. Those were actually commendable things.

In fact, this particular individual was going above and beyond what the law required. It was customary for a man to tithe from his crops, but this Pharisee did more than that—he tithed everything. Should we criticize him for this when we ourselves seldom tithe even a part of what of what we own? Or should we criticize him for fasting twice a week when we ourselves don't fast even once a month or once a year? We defend ourselves by saying we're now living by grace, not law—that we're under the New Covenant, not the Old Covenant. But having a proper understanding of the New Covenant means you'll give *more* than you would under the law, not less; you'll fast and pray *more,* not less.

The point Jesus was making was not that the Pharisee was wrong to do these things, but that he *trusted* in what he was doing—he trusted in himself.

We can do the same thing. We think, *God's going to hear me because I went to church this Sunday—that has to mean something to Him.* Or *God is sure to hear me because I spent a lot of time in personal Bible study this morning* or *because I shared the gospel with someone last week* or *because lately I've been helping a lot of other people*—or even *because I've been wrestling so intensely in prayer.*

No, God will hear you today and every day only because you come to Him through Jesus Christ, through His shed blood, and not for any other reason. He hears our prayers because of the sacrifice of Jesus.

Lost and Valuable

Not only was the praying Pharisee trusting in himself, but it appears he was praying loudly so that everyone around would hear and be impressed.

And notice especially the attitude he conveyed toward the tax collector: "I thank You that I'm not like...*this tax collector.*" His words seem to drip with disdain. And you know, as Jesus told this story, most of the people who were listening probably felt the same way toward tax collectors. It's an attitude so many of us can have toward non-Christians.

It concerns me when I hear believers speaking of non-believers as the enemy. According to Scripture, those who do not believe have been taken captive by Satan to do his will—they're prisoners of war. Nonbelievers aren't the enemy; they're the enemy's captives. And it wasn't all that long ago that you were right there in prison with them, bound by your sin and without the Savior.

We need to have compassion for nonbelievers, not condescension, because you're never going to effectively share your faith with people if you don't first care about them.

The tax collector in Jesus' story was indeed a bad guy. But he still needed the Savior.

Remember how Jesus dealt with another tax collector named Zacchaeus? We know Zacchaeus enriched himself off of the misery of others. But when Jesus (in Luke 19) was walking through town and spotted this hated man up in a tree, He stopped and looked up and said, "Zacchaeus, come down—we're going to have a meal together!"

Can you imagine the shock Zacchaeus felt? And the shock felt by all the people in the street who heard Jesus say this? They would likely have cheered if Jesus had spotted Zacchaeus up there and called out, "Hey, everybody, let's set fire to the tree!"

But Jesus had compassion. He was immediately criticized for it, but He said, "The Son of Man has come to seek and to save that which was lost" (Luke 19:10).

People who are lost have value to God. They're uniquely created in His image. He loves them enough to have sent His own Son to die on the cross for them. We need to see these people not as the Pharisee would see them, but as Jesus would see them—as sheep without a shepherd.

Me, the Sinner
Now let's take a closer look at this bad guy, the tax collector. What a contrast!

> And the tax collector, standing afar off, would not
> so much as raise his eyes to heaven, but beat his
> breast, saying, "God be merciful to me a sinner!"
> (18:13)

Instead of announcing his virtues in the way the Pharisee did, this man confessed his sins. He had no desire to compare himself with the Pharisee or with anybody else. He knew he fell far short of God's standards, and he took total responsibility for his acts. He made no excuses; there was no shifting of blame.

He prayed the only real sinner's prayer I know of in the Bible: "God be merciful to me a sinner!" The phrase he used, "to me a sinner," can also be translated, "to me *the* sinner." Not just one of many sinners, but *the* sinner! This tax collector must have been notorious for his wickedness.

The apostle Paul made a similar statement when he wrote, "Christ Jesus came into the world to save sinners, *of whom I am chief*" (1 Timothy 1:15). That brings up an interesting point: The closer you get to God and the more you become like Jesus, *the more aware you become of your sinful nature.*

Which means that the more critical you are of others, the less spiritual you really are. And the more spiritual you are, the less critical you'll be—because you genuinely realize that you're certainly no better, and probably even worse, than those around you.

The godly men and women I've had the privilege of getting to know over the years have always been humble people, not full of themselves. Show me a person who always has a critical word for somebody else, always nit-picking this or that about someone else, and I'll show you a person full of pharisaical pride.

Jesus made His point loud and clear concerning the tax collector:

> I tell you, this man went down to his house justi-fied rather than the other; for everyone who exalts himself will be abased, and he who humbles him-self will be exalted. (Luke 18:14)

In wrestling prayer, we must not forget that the way of approaching God that's commended by Christ is the pathway of humility taken by this tax collector: "God be merci-ful to me the sinner!"

Humble yourself under the mighty hand of God, and then, even on the wrestling mat, He will lift you up.

Chapter Seven

IT'S ALL ABOUT
RELATIONSHIP

For this final chapter on wrestling with God, I want to take us back to the very first thing Jesus said in the model prayer that He gave us. Jesus told us to begin by saying, "Our Father...."

Now that happens to be a very noteworthy beginning. To think so intimately of God as our Father was a revolutionary thought to the Jewish mind. The Jews feared God and attached such sacredness to God's name that they wouldn't even utter it aloud. That's why when Jesus referred to God as His Father, they accused Him of blasphemy. But now, because of His death on the cross, we, too, can call God our Father.

It's true that God is to be reverenced. He's all-powerful, all-knowing, and present everywhere. He's ignorant of nothing, unlimited in power, and not bound by time and space. And He's absolutely righteous and holy.

And this same holy and awesome God is *our Father!* He's not unapproachable, disinterested, or preoccupied. Rather, He wants to enjoy intimacy with each of us, His children. As our Father, He is totally fair, good, and loving. His decisions and purposes for our lives are always right, just, proper, and always motivated by pure goodness and a deep and abiding love for us.

When my oldest son, Christopher, was a little boy, I would take him to toy stores, which both of us liked to visit. It was never all that hard for me to decide what toys he or his younger brother Jonathan would like—I simply picked what I personally enjoyed playing with. I guess I'm still a kid at heart in some ways.

On those occasions when Christopher and I were visiting the toy store, I would say, "Go ahead, son, pick out something for yourself." He would be looking at some inexpensive action figure, while I would more likely be eyeing the battery-operated tank that the action figure would drive.

He would tell me his choice, and then I would point to the tank and say, "Maybe this one would be more fun!" And the bigger toy is the one we would get. I know I was probably spoiling him, but I loved to do unexpected things for him like that. And eventually when we visited toy stores and I told him to pick out something, he would wisely respond, "Dad, why don't you choose for me?" Christopher came to realize that my choices for him were better than his choices for himself.

That's true of our heavenly Father as well. Don't be afraid to say, "Lord, choose for me!"

After all, Father knows best.

The fact that we could have the privilege of even approaching a God like this is staggering! What else can we say to such a revelation but "Hallowed be Your name!" And for us to be called His son or daughter means that our wrestling in prayer must always come down to growing in our relationship with Him as our Father.

Every Right

What right do we have to approach God Almighty with our human needs?

We have every right—because Jesus told us to! Later in the model prayer, He teaches us to pray, "Give us this day our daily bread" (Matthew 6:11). That's how intimately God wants to be involved with us.

Why would God be concerned about what concerns us? Why would He care about my needs and my wants? Why would He commit Himself personally to providing my daily bread?

Many reasons could be cited, but the most notable

would simply be that He loves you and He loves me. Just as an earthly parent loves to give gifts to his or her children, so does our heavenly Father.

To ask for our daily bread is not only making our needs known; it's also an affirmation that everything we have ultimately comes from Him. "Every good gift and every perfect gift is from above, and comes down from the Father of lights" (James 1:17).

God Almighty has committed Himself personally to meeting the needs of His children. "He who did not spare His own Son, but delivered Him up for us all, how shall He not with Him also freely give us all things?" (Romans 8:32). So by all means, bring your personal needs and requests to God.

And as you do so—especially in wrestling prayer where perhaps you're pushing forward by faith to ask for something bigger than you've ever requested before—remember to check your motives. Wrong motives keep us from receiving God's gifts. "When you ask, you do not receive, because you ask with wrong motives, that you may spend what you get on your pleasures" (James 4:3, NIV).

We may be praying, "Lord use me!" but why are we praying such a prayer? Is it really for His glory or our own? Do we see ourselves in the spotlight, surrounded by people who've come to hear us teach or preach or sing? Do we want to hear people speaking our name?

Or perhaps our motive behind such a request is simply a desire for our own ease and comfort, even at the expense of what's best for others around us. If that kind of thinking is ultimately at the root of our request, don't count on God to go along with it.

The Hardest Part

When we're truly wrestling in prayer, pushing forward in our relationship as a son or daughter with God the Father, eventually we must come to the point of acknowledging our sinfulness and allowing God to deal with it by His grace and forgiveness—a process that also requires our forgiveness of others.

This may well be the part of prayer where you wrestle most!

Some Christians think they don't need forgiveness now that they have been saved. But according to the model prayer that Jesus gave us, it's something we should be asking for on a regular basis: "And forgive us our debts, as we forgive our debtors" (Matthew 6:12). Or as it's expressed in Luke, "And forgive us our sins, for we also forgive everyone who is indebted to us" (Luke 11:4). This covers our sins, our trespasses, our shortcomings, our resentments—all the wrong things we've done.

"If we say that we have no sin," John tells us, "we deceive ourselves, and the truth is not in us" (1 John 1:8).

Those who don't see constant need for regular cleansing are not spending much time in God's presence, for the more we contemplate the holiness of God, the more we will see our own sinfulness.

It's interesting to look at Paul's view of himself across the span of his writings. He went from describing himself as the "least of the apostles" in 1 Corinthians 15:9 to "the least of all the saints" in Ephesians 3:8 to the chief of sinners in 1 Timothy 1:15. Now that's spiritual growth! The greater the saint, the greater the awareness of sin within.

No matter how intense or fervent or long your prayers may be, if you have unconfessed sin in your life, your prayers are really going nowhere. "If I regard iniquity in my heart, the Lord will not hear" (Psalm 66:18). It may be some sin in your past that has remained unjudged and unconfessed. God can't forgive the sin you won't confess.

Or it may be something you're doing now that you don't consider to be sin, but God has a different take on it. It's good to pray as David prayed:

Search me, O God, and know my heart;
    Try me, and know my anxieties;
And see if there is any wicked way in me,
    And lead me in the way everlasting.
(Psalm 139:23–24)

The Proof of Forgiveness

While you're seeking God's forgiveness, you must also forgive others. This aspect of Christ's teaching is very important and often missed. The "proof" that you and I are forgiven and that we've accepted that forgiveness is that *we forgive others!* The man who knows he has been forgiven must be willing to extend forgiveness to those who have wronged *him.*

In many ways forgiveness is the key to all relationships that are healthy, strong, and lasting. Because as fatally flawed people, we *will* sin. We're going to hurt one another, whether intentionally or unintentionally. Husbands will offend wives, and wives will offend husbands. Parents will hurt their children, and children will hurt their parents. Family members will upset one another, neighbors will offend neighbors, and friends will hurt friends. That's why we must learn to forgive.

> *Forgiveness is the key to healthy, strong, and lasting relationships.*

When there's no forgiveness, a "root of bitterness" grows (Hebrews 12:15), and when a root of bitterness takes hold, that's the end of the relationship.

Our society today doesn't like forgiveness. We exalt vengeance and violence instead. If someone cuts you off on the freeway, then by all means speed up, pass him, and cut *him* off to get even. If your neighbor upsets you, sue him! I read a true account of a little three-year-old girl named Nina who was playing in a sandbox when another three-year-old, Jonathan, ran up and kicked her. Nina's mother scolded this boy sternly. Jonathan's mother yelled at Nina's mother. So Nina's mother then sued Jonathan's mother and had a restraining order issued.

But Jesus is telling us that as forgiven people, we must be forgiving people. Our generous and constant forgiveness of others should be the natural result of our embracing the forgiveness God has extended to us. Paul tells us, "Be kind to one another, tenderhearted, forgiving one another, just as God in Christ also forgave you" (Ephesians 4:32).

How Do We Do the Impossible?

Maybe you already realize this—you already know you must forgive—but actually doing it is so difficult! There's someone you need to forgive in your heart, but doing so is the biggest struggle you will face as you wrestle in prayer. How can we possibly forgive others as Christ forgave us?

Only by the help of the Holy Spirit.

But we must take that first step. Don't wait until you feel like it. Just do it.

In her book *The Hiding Place*, Corrie ten Boom tells about speaking at a church service in Germany, where after the service she was approached by a man whom she quickly recognized. It was one of the Nazi soldiers who had stood guard at the shower room door when she and her sister were brought into a German concentration camp. Suddenly her mind was flooded with the memory of this man and others mocking her and her sister and the other naked women prisoners.

With his hand extended, the former guard thanked her for her message about our sins being washed away in Christ. But she couldn't bring herself to return his greeting.

> I, who had preached so often to the people the need to forgive, kept my hand at my side. Even as the angry, vengeful thoughts boiled through me, I saw the sin of them.

> Jesus Christ had died for this man; was I going to ask for more? *Lord Jesus,* I prayed, *forgive me and help me to forgive him.* I tried to smile; I struggled to raise my hand. I could not. I felt nothing, not the slightest spark of warmth or charity. And so again I breathed a silent prayer. *Jesus, I cannot forgive him. Give me Your forgiveness.*

> As I took his hand the most incredible thing happened. From my shoulder along my arm and through my hand a current seemed to pass from

me to him, while into my heart sprang a love for
this stranger that almost overwhelmed me.

And so I discovered that it is not on our forgiveness any more than on our goodness that the
world's healing hinges, but on His.

AFTER THE WRESTLING, REST

Finally, remember that your relationship with God your
heavenly Father is not primarily one of wrestling, but of
rest.

Rejoice and relax in the incredible truth that "having
been justified by faith, we have peace with God through
our Lord Jesus Christ" (Romans 5:1). This peace is *real*
peace, something that we have and can enjoy *now.*

Remember what Corrie ten Boom also said: "Don't
wrestle; just nestle!"

Yes, it's true that sometimes we go through periods of
deep spiritual struggle before we can break through to new
and deeper awareness and enjoyment of God. And I
encourage you to go forth boldly and confidently into those
times and seasons of spiritual struggle, fully intending to get
all you can out of them and to learn all you can.

But the breakthrough must come. Don't let the struggle keep you burdened with heaviness. "Come to Me,"
Jesus says, "all you who labor and are heavy laden, and I will

give you *rest*" (Matthew 11:28). That invitation is *always* open.

Meanwhile, I urge you especially to be committed to persevering, wrestling prayer for the salvation of unbelievers around you.

Knowing that the Lord is "not willing that any should perish but that all should come to repentance" (2 Peter 3:9), George Müeller as a young man began praying daily for the conversion of a friend and kept praying persistently. Very late in his life he wrote, "I have been praying for sixty-three years and eight months for one man's conversion. He is not converted yet, but he will be! How can it be otherwise? There is the unchanging promise of Jehovah, and on that I rest."

When George Müeller died, the man was still unsaved—but before Müeller was buried, his friend was converted! God answered Müeller's persevering prayer, and He will also answer yours.

The publisher and author would love to hear your comments about this book. *Please contact us at:* www.lifechangebooks.com

The Treasure Principle
Discovering the Secret of Joyful Giving
Randy Alcorn ISBN 1-57673-780-2

Bestselling author Randy Alcorn uncovers the revolutionary key to spiritual transformation: joyful giving! Jesus gave his followers this life-changing formula that guarantees not only kingdom impact, but immediate pleasure and eternal rewards.

The Treasure Principle Bible Study ISBN 1-59052-187-0

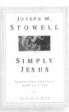

Simply Jesus
Experiencing the One Your Heart Longs For
Joseph M. Stowell ISBN 1-57673-856-6

Simplify your life! Let temptation, trouble, and surrender cut away religious formulas and lead you toward simple companionship with Jesus Christ! Moody Bible College president Joe Stowell shows how.

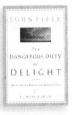

The Dangerous Duty of Delight
The Glorified God and the Satisfied Soul
John Piper ISBN 1-57673-883-3

Strengthen your relationship with God by enjoying Him and His creation! Discover just how to delight in the Lord in this compact version of Piper's classic *Desiring God*.

Certain Peace in Uncertain Times
Embracing Prayer in an Anxious Age
Shirley Dobson ISBN 1-57673-937-6

Respond to a chaotic world with inner peace and resolve. National Day of Prayer Task Force chairman Shirley Dobson shows you how to nurture a true and lasting lifestyle of prayer.

SMALL BOOKS
BIG CHANGE

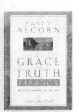